Bella is happy. She has a red felt tip pen.

She puts a big red spot
on her chin.

Then she puts lots of red spots on her cheeks.

Tom sees the red spots on Bella's chin and cheeks.

'Bella, will you put red
spots on me?' says Tom.

Bella puts red spots on Tom's cheeks and chin.

'Look we have spots,' says Tom to Mum.

Mum tells Tom and Bella
to jump in the bath.